CREATIVE ⬥ EDUCATION

NEW YORK
KNICKS

AARON FRISCH

Published by Creative Education
P.O. Box 227
Mankato, Minnesota 56002
Creative Education is an imprint of The Creative Company.

DESIGN AND PRODUCTION BY **ZENO DESIGN**

PHOTOGRAPHS BY Corbis (Frank Mastro),
Getty Images (NBAE)

LIBRARY OF CONGRESS CATALOGING-IN-PUBLICATION DATA

Frisch, Aaron.
New York Knicks / by Aaron Frisch.
p. cm. — (NBA champions)
Includes index.
ISBN-13: 978-1-58341-509-2
1. New York Knickerbockers (Basketball team)—History.
2. Basketball—History. I. Title.

GV885.52.N4F75 2007
796.323'64097471—dc22   2006020242

First edition

9 8 7 6 5 4 3 2 1

COVER PHOTO: *Guard Steve Francis*

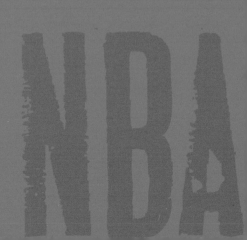

CREATIVE EDUCATION

CHAMPIONS

CREATIVE EDUCATION

4

THE KNICKS are a professional basketball team in the National Basketball Association (NBA). They play in New York City. New York is the biggest city in the United States. More than eight million people live there!

New York is sometimes called "The Big Apple" ▷

5

6

THE KNICKS' arena is called Madison Square Garden. Their uniforms are blue, orange, and white. The Knicks play lots of games against teams called the 76ers, Celtics, Nets, and Raptors.

◁ Madison Square Garden is a very famous arena

7

8

THE KNICKS played their first season in 1946. Their first great player was a forward named Carl Braun *[BRON]*. He was good at both basketball and baseball.

Carl Braun played 12 seasons with the Knicks ▷

9

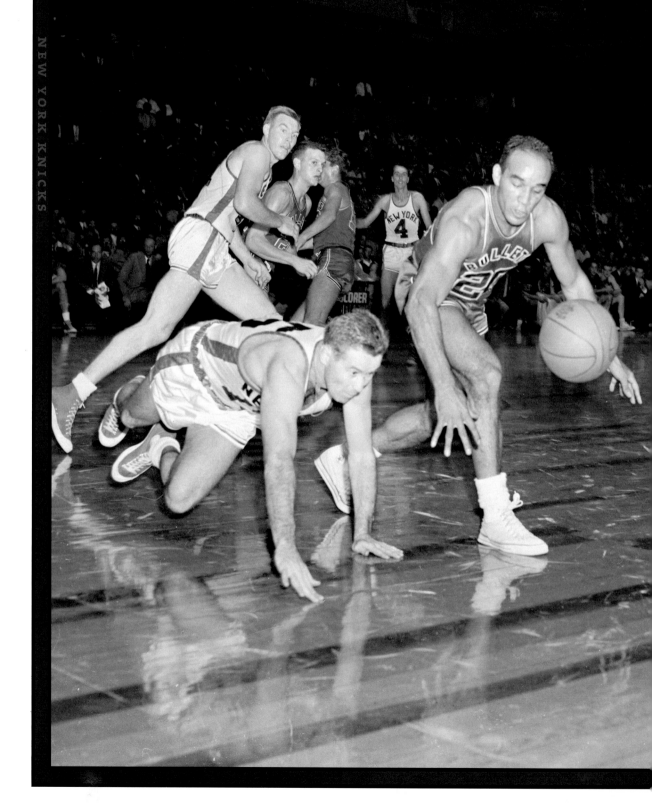

THE KNICKS were a great team in the 1950s. Their players were not very tall, but they were quick. Fans called them the "New York Five." They came close to winning the NBA championship three times.

◁ The Knicks were a fast team in the 1950s

11

IN 1967, the Knicks got a smart coach named Red Holzman. The team had some new players, too. Willis Reed was a strong forward. Walt "Clyde" Frazier was a fast guard with great all-around skills.

Walt Frazier was a fan favorite in New York ▷

NBA CHAMPIONS 1970 1973

13

14

REED and Frazier helped the Knicks win their first NBA championship in 1970. In the last game, Reed played even though his leg was hurt. New York fans thought he was a hero. Three years later, the Knicks won the championship again.

15

◁ Willis Reed helped make the Knicks champions

16

AFTER THAT, the Knicks got other star players. Bernard King was a forward with a great jump shot. Patrick Ewing *[YOO-wing]* was a tough center who played 15 seasons for the Knicks.

Bernard King could leap high to shoot the ball ▷

17

18

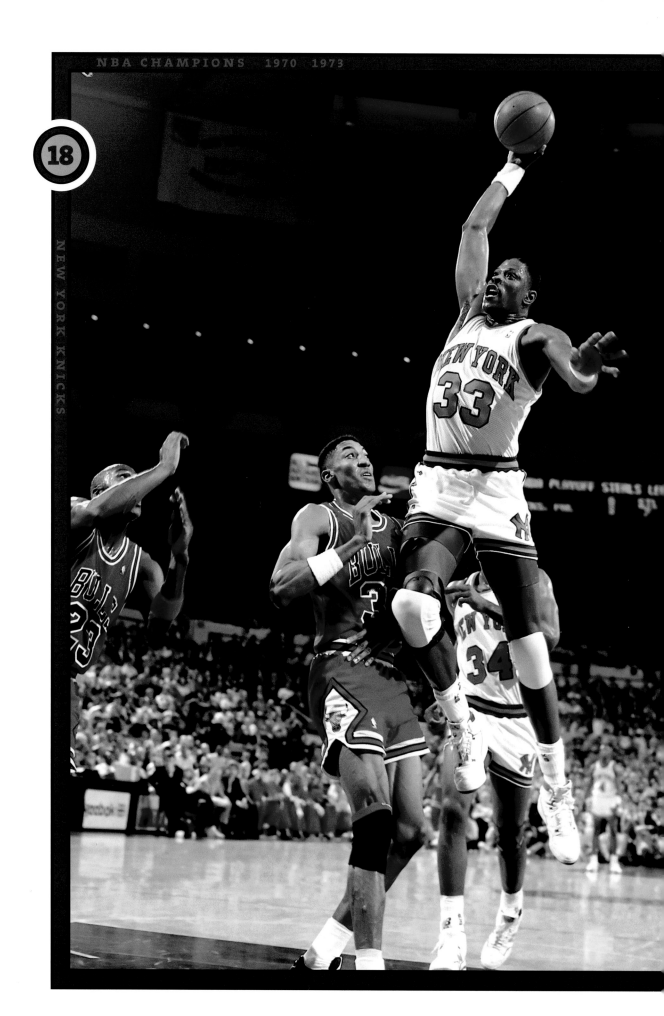

EWING helped the Knicks make the playoffs many times in the 1990s. In 1994, they needed to win only one game against a team called the Rockets to win the championship. But New York lost.

19

◁ Patrick Ewing was a great player for many years

20

STEPHON MARBURY was another good Knicks player. He was a quick point guard who scored a lot. The Knicks have many new players today. New York fans hope that their team will win the NBA championship again soon!

Stephon Marbury grew up in New York ▷

NBA CHAMPIONS 1970 1973

21

GLOSSARY

ARENA   a building with lots of seats where teams play basketball

NATIONAL BASKETBALL ASSOCIATION (NBA)
a group of basketball teams that play against each other; there are 30 teams in the NBA today

PLAYOFFS   games that are played after the season to see which team is the best

PROFESSIONAL   a person or team that gets paid to play or work

FUN FACTS

TEAM COLORS: Blue, orange, and white

HOME ARENA: Madison Square Garden

CONFERENCE/DIVISION: Eastern Conference, Atlantic Division

FIRST SEASON: 1946

NBA CHAMPIONSHIPS: 1970, 1973

GREAT PLAYERS: Carl Braun (guard), Walt Frazier (guard), Patrick Ewing (center)

NBA WEB SITE FOR KIDS: http://www.nba.com/kids/

TEAM NAME: The Knicks got their name because people in New York used to wear short pants called knickerbockers. "Knicks" is short for knickerbockers.

23

24

INDEX